A Kid's Guide to Drawing America™

How to Dr

Alaska's
Sights and Symbols

Jennifer Quasha

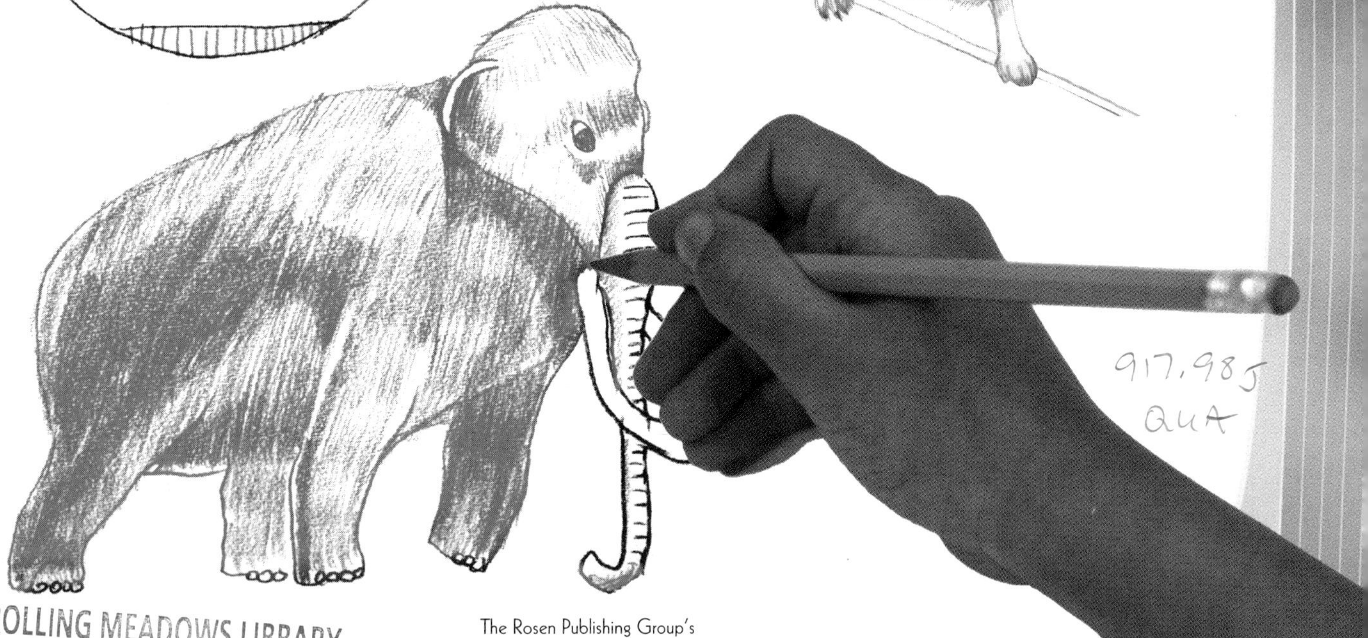

The Rosen Publishing Group's
PowerKids Press™
New York

Published in 2002 by The Rosen Publishing Group, Inc.
29 East 21st Street, New York, NY 10010

First Edition

Book and Layout Design: Kim Sonsky
Project Editor: Jannell Khu

Illustration Credits: Laura Murawski
Photo Credits: Title page (hand) by Arlan Dean; p. 7 © Galen Rowell/CORBIS; pp. 8 (photo), 8 (sketch), 9 (painting) Courtesy of Anchorage Museum of History and Art; p. 12 © One Mile Up, Incorporated; p. 14 by Kim Sonsky; p. 16 © Andy Small/CORBIS; p. 18 © Tom Bean/CORBIS; p. 20 © Kennan Ward/CORBIS; pp. 22, 26 © IndexStock; p. 24 © Jonathan Blair/CORBIS; p. 28 © James Marshall/CORBIS.

Quasha, Jennifer.
How to draw Alaska's sights and symbols / Jennifer Quasha.
p. cm. —(A kid's guide to drawing America)
Includes index.
Summary: This book describes how to draw some of Alaska's sights and symbols, including the state's seal, the state's flag, Mount McKinley, and others.
    ISBN 0-8239-6056-0
1. Emblems, State—Alaska—Juvenile literature.   2. Alaska in art—Juvenile literature. 3. Drawing—Technique—Juvenile literature. [1. Emblems, State—Alaska. 2. Alaska. 3. Drawing—Technique] I. Title. II. Series.
2001
    743'.8'09798—dc21

Manufactured in the United States of America

CONTENTS

1	Let's Draw Alaska	4
2	The Great Land	6
3	Artist in Alaska	8
4	Map of Alaska	10
5	The State Seal	12
6	The State Flag	14
7	The Forget-Me-Not	16
8	The Sitka Spruce	18
9	The Willow Ptarmigan	20
10	The Giant King Salmon	22
11	The Woolly Mammoth	24
12	Mount McKinley	26
13	Alaska's Capitol	28
	Alaska State Facts	30
	Glossary	31
	Index	32
	Web Sites	32

Let's Draw Alaska

The LasI Frontier is one of Alaska's nicknames. This nickname perfectly describes Alaska because there are many areas that are remote and that have not been spoiled by development. However, more and more tourists are visiting Alaska. Some popular places to visit are Katmai National Park and Preserve, the Aleutian Islands, and the Sitka National Historic Park. Helicopter tours to see the state's many magnificent ice fields and glaciers are also popular.

Alaska's state motto, North to the Future, represents Alaska as a land of promise. Alaska leads all other states in the volume of fish production. Salmon is one of the state's leading products. The discovery of oil in the Kenai Peninsula in 1957 has helped to make Alaska a wealthy state. Alaska also has large reserves of gold, nickel, tin, lead, and copper.

With this book, you will learn about some of Alaska's exciting sights and symbols and how to draw them! All of the drawings start with a simple shape. From there you will keep adding other shapes. Under every drawing, directions help explain how to do the step. Each new step of the drawing is shown in red to help guide you. You can check out the drawing terms and illustrations on this page for help. The last step of most of the drawings is to add shading. To shade, just tilt your pencil to the side and hold it with your index finger. You also can leave your drawings unshaded.

These are the supplies you will need to draw Alaska's sights and symbols:

- A sketch pad
- An eraser
- A number 2 pencil
- A pencil sharpener

These are some of the shapes and drawing terms you need to know to draw Alaska's sights and symbols:

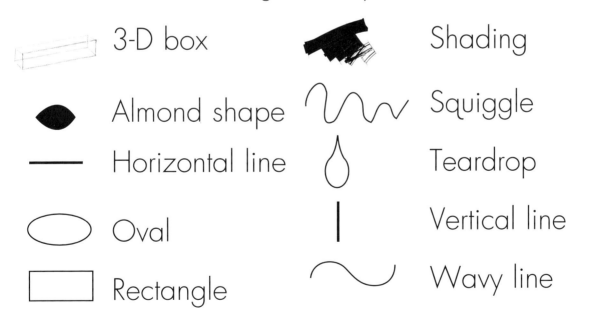

3-D box

Almond shape

Horizontal line

Oval

Rectangle

Shading

Squiggle

Teardrop

Vertical line

Wavy line

The Great Land

Alaska is the biggest state in America. It is more than twice the size of Texas, which is the second-largest state. Alaska covers more than 615,000 square miles (1,592,843 sq km) of land. For such a big state, Alaska has the second-smallest population in the United States, with only about 614,000 people. Juneau is the capital of Alaska and about 30,684 people live there. The city with the largest population is Anchorage, where more than 250,500 people live.

Alaska was one of the last states to join the nation. On January 3, 1959, it was made the forty-ninth state. One of Alaska's nicknames is the Great Land because the name "Alaska" comes from the word *alaxsxaq*. This translates to "great land," or "mainland," in Aleut. Aleut is a native Alaskan language. The state of Alaska has the farthest northern, eastern, and western points of land in the United States.

An Inuit woman and children in winter furs stand on the ice shelf at Barrow, Alaska, the northernmost city in the United States.

Artist in Alaska

Even though Sydney Laurence didn't move to Alaska until he was 38 years old, he is one of Alaska's most famous artists. Laurence was born in Brooklyn, New York, in 1865. He studied painting in New York City, and then in Paris at the École des Beaux Arts. In 1903,

This photo of Sydney Laurence in his Anchorage art studio was taken around 1927.

Laurence moved to Juneau, Alaska, to work as a photographer. Laurence didn't start painting seriously until 1913. He was especially interested in painting landscapes of his adopted home. From 1925 until his death in 1940, Laurence spent his summers in Alaska to sketch Alaska's incredible landscapes. He then spent winters in Los

This is one of Sydney Laurence's sketches of Mount McKinley. The sketch was done in pencil on paper.

Angeles, California, and transformed his sketches into beautiful landscape paintings.

Laurence's paintings were influenced by the impressionists, a group of painters in Paris during the nineteenth century. Impressionists relied on the beauty of light and painted directly from nature rather than from imagination. Laurence's use of light and his focus to paint nature realistically was also influenced by a school of painting called luminism. Luminist painters were American painters who painted grand landscapes full of light and nature unspoiled by development. The painting shown here, entitled *Mt. McKinley*, is influenced by both impressionism and luminism.

Laurence's painting *Mt. McKinley*, done in oil on canvas, is 19⅝" x 15½" (49 cm x 39 cm). He painted this famous mountain rising above the Tokositna River around 1930.

Map of Alaska

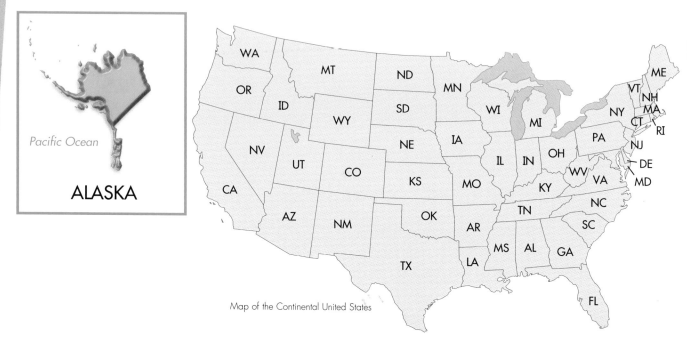

Pacific Ocean

ALASKA

Map of the Continental United States

Most of Alaska's eastern border is a straight line, which borders Canada's Yukon Territory. Western Alaska's coast is broken up by the Seward Peninsula, which juts out and is separated from Russia by the Bering Strait. That point in Alaska is only 53 miles (85 km) from Russia! Alaska is a huge peninsula with two long strips of land that jut out like legs. The right "leg" is 500 miles (805 km) long and borders British Columbia. Alaska's left leg is formed by the Alaska Peninsula and the Aleutian Island chain, which stretches southwest. Alaska's coast touches many bodies of water, the Arctic Ocean, the Chukchi Sea, the Bering Sea, the Pacific Ocean, and the Gulf of Alaska.

1

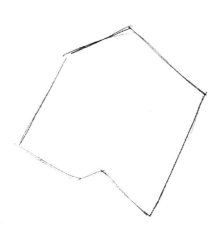

Draw the angled shape as shown.

2

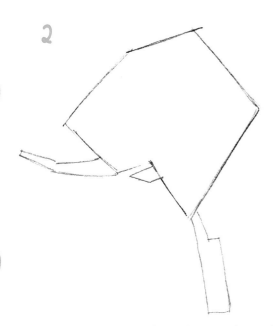

Underneath the first shape, draw three smaller, angled shapes as shown. Study the shapes carefully before you begin the drawings.

3

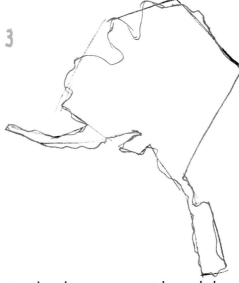

Use the shape as a guide and draw ragged edges as shown. Erase the straight lines. You may need to redraw the ragged edges. Now let's draw some of Alaska's important places!

4

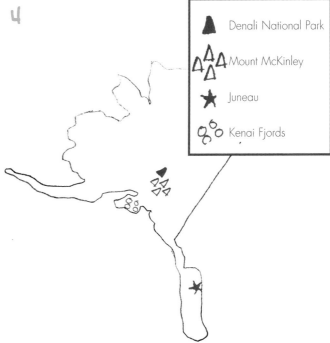

a. For Juneau, the state capital, draw a five-pointed star in the lower right strip of land as shown.

b. Draw a triangle toward the center of the state. Shade in the triangle. This is the Denali National Park.

c. For Mount McKinley, draw little triangles underneath Denali National Park.

d. Draw little circles below Mount McKinley. These are the Kenai Fjords.

The State Seal

The state seal of Alaska was designed in 1913, when Alaska was a territory and not a state. It became an official state seal in 1960, a year after Alaska became a state. There are many images on the state seal which represent the many important parts of Alaska. Alaska's many mountains and icebergs are shown in the distance, and the rays that shine behind them are the sky's northern lights. On the left side is a mining factory, as well as a dock and a ship. These represent Alaska's shipping and mining industries. In the foreground, horses are pulling a farmer on a sled. This stands for the state's rich agriculture. Around the seal is a band that reads "The Seal of the State of Alaska" and also shows two images, one of a fish and one of two seals. The fish and the seals represent Alaska's rich wildlife and fishing industries.

1

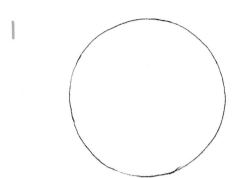

Draw a circle.

2

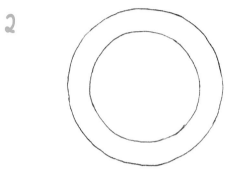

Draw another, smaller circle within the first circle.

3

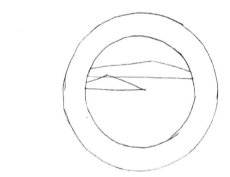

Draw the flat, triangular shapes in the circle as shown. These are the mountains.

4

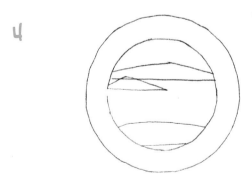

Draw two horizontal lines at the bottom. This is the land.

5

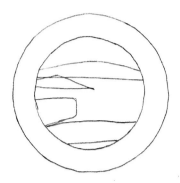

Draw the shape as shown. This is where the trees will be drawn later.

6

Put curves in the mountains. Add lines above the mountains for the sun rays.

7

Add lines in the area between the shapes for the water. Draw little triangles with a curved line underneath. These are the ships.

8

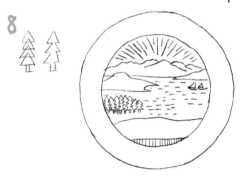

Finish by drawing the trees. Add the details as shown. Good job!

13

The State Flag

The Alaskan state flag was designed in 1926 by a thirteen-year-old boy named Benny Benson. The flag was officially recognized in 1927. Benny won a statewide contest that was held for students in grades seven through twelve. His flag design was chosen from 142 entries.

The flag design is simple but has many meanings. The flag has eight gold stars on a dark blue background. The blue represents the Alaskan sky in the evening, the many bodies of water that surround the state, and Alaska's blue forget-me-not flower. The gold stars represent gold, which was found in Alaska during the Klondike gold rush. The seven gold stars also form the constellation the Big Dipper, or the Great Bear. The Great Bear symbolizes strength. The large star is the North Star and stands for Alaska's future.

1

Begin by drawing a rectangle. This is the basic shape of the flag.

2

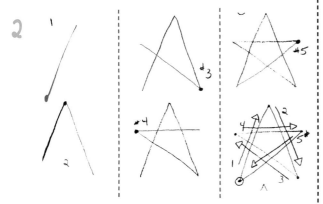

On a piece of scrap paper, practice drawing a five-pointed star. Pay attention to the red lines. Draw the red lines in the order shown from 1 through 5.

3

You are now ready to draw a five-pointed star in the upper right corner of the rectangle.

4

Now draw four smaller five-pointed stars. Pay attention to the placement of these stars. Notice that they go up toward the left corner of the flag.

5

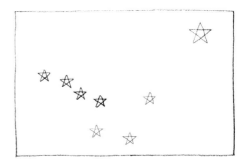

Draw three more five-pointed stars as shown.

6

Shade or color in the area around the stars. Hold your pencil on its side and gently stroke the paper. You just finished drawing Alaska's state flag!

15

The Forget-Me-Not

   In 1949, the forget-me-not flower became Alaska's state flower. Forget-me-nots grow wild all over Alaska. The flower has a yellow center and is surrounded by five blue petals. Many flowers grow on each stem. Forget-me-nots are perennial flowers, which means that they can grow for several years without having to be replanted. Forget-me-nots have been well loved since the first pioneers came to the state of Alaska. There is a poem about Alaska's state flower. We may not know who wrote this poem, but we do know that the person loved the forget-me-not flower:

A little flower blossoms forth
On every hill and dale,
The emblem of the Pioneers
Upon the rugged trail;
The Pioneers have asked it
And we could deny them not;
So the emblem of Alaska
Is the blue Forget-me-not.

1

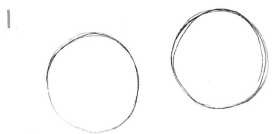

Begin by drawing two circles. These are the basic shapes of the flowers.

2

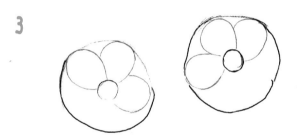

Draw a smaller circle in the center of each circle.

3

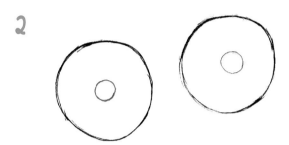

You are ready to draw the petals. Draw balloonlike shapes extending from the centers. Notice how each petal overlaps the next petal.

4

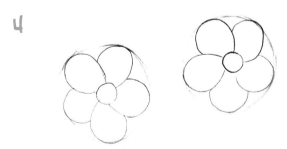

Work on the first petals and draw a few more. Notice how they spiral around the center of the flower. You should have five petals on each flower.

5

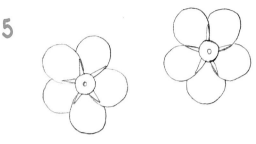

Draw little circles in the center of each flower. Next draw small triangles at the edge of the petals as shown.

6

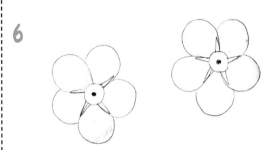

Start shading the petals. Turn your pencil on its side and gently stroke the paper. Shade in the little circle in the center of the flowers.

7

Continue shading by pressing harder on your pencil. Work slowly and lightly. Gradually shade in the drawing. Notice how the areas toward the center and around the triangles are the darkest. Great job!

The Sitka Spruce

The sitka spruce became Alaska's state tree in 1962. It is the world's biggest and fastest-growing spruce tree and grows in southeastern and central Alaska. Sitka spruce trees can reach 300 feet (91 m) in height and 15 feet (5 m) in diameter. The tree's dark green needles are flat and sharp and can grow up to 1 inch (2.5 cm) long. The tree grows orange and brown cones which are 2–3 inches (5–8 cm) long. The tree's roots can be made into ropes, hats, fishing lines, nets, and baskets. Today the sitka spruce wood is used to make musical instruments such as guitars!

1

Draw a tall, thin triangle. This is the trunk.

2

Draw lines on either side of the trunk. Notice that the branches are longer as you go down the trunk.

3

Turn your pencil on its side and lightly shade from side to side on top of the trunk. Shade up and down along the branches with short, gentle stokes. Hold the pencil lightly while you stroke the paper gently.

4

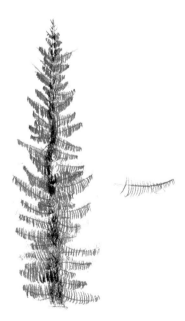

To draw the needles, darken the shaded areas. Begin at the end of the branch and draw small lines that get gradually larger toward the center. Finish shading the trunk by turning your pencil on its side again. Great job!

The Willow Ptarmigan

The willow ptarmigan, also known as the willow grouse, became Alaska's state bird in 1955. Willow ptarmigans like to stay in flocks, or groups, and they shy away from humans. The male and female birds have different coloring. The male willow ptarmigans have reddish foreheads, crowns, and napes, and the females are light brown all over. Males are about 17 inches (43 cm) long and weigh about 1.25 pounds (.57 kg), and females are 16 inches (41 cm) long and weigh about 1 pound (.45 kg). Young ptarmigans have light-colored feathers until the birds reach two years old. In the winter, the ptarmigan grows hairlike feathers on its feet, which allow them to glide across the snow. In the winter, their feathers turn white to blend in with the snowy landscape.

Draw a circle. This is the body of the bird.

2

Draw a curved shape extending from the circle. This is the neck and head of the bird.

3

Draw two small circles underneath the first circle. Draw two lines connecting the lower circle. These are the feet and one leg.

4

Draw a triangle on the side of the bigger circle. This is the tail.

5

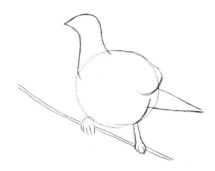

Draw the wing as shown. Now draw in the feet and the branch. Good job.

6

Draw the beak and eye. Draw the outline of the feathers on the neck as shown.

7

Continue drawing the feathers on the neck and back. For the tiny feathers, draw little semicircles that overlap. Shade in the tail.

8

Finish shading the head, neck, wing, and feet of the bird. Shade lightly and work slowly.

The Giant King Salmon

The giant king salmon became Alaska's state fish on March 25, 1962. Giant king salmon weigh, on an average, 20 pounds (9 kg), but some can weigh up to 100 pounds (45 kg)! Salmon fish eggs hatch in a river. Salmon swim to the sea and live there for some time, then migrate back to familiar rivers to lay eggs.

There are more than 3,000 rivers and more than 3 million lakes in Alaska. The largest lake is Lake Iliamna, which covers more than 1,000 square miles (2,590 sq km). With all of these lakes and rivers, there is an abundance of seafood in Alaska. Salmon is an important cash product for Alaska. Alaskans export salmon to the rest of the United States and to other seafood-loving countries in Asia and Europe.

1

Draw the fish shape as shown.

2

Draw a curved line on the left side. This is the head. Draw triangle shapes on either side of the fish. These are the fins.

3

Draw a small circle for the eye. Draw in the mouth and the lines on the face as shown.

4

Shade in the eye. Add a horizontal line across the body.

5

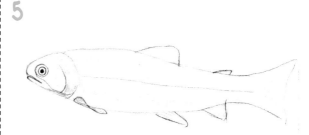

Begin shading lightly. Lightly shade the entire fish except for areas in the head.

6

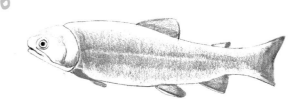

Continue shading. Notice how the area in the center is the darkest part of the body. Now shade the fins even darker than the body. Excellent!

The Woolly Mammoth

The woolly mammoth became Alaska's state fossil in 1986. These animals lived during the Ice Age, between 1.8 million and 11,000 years ago. Alaska was one place they lived. An entire woolly mammoth was found frozen in ice in Siberia, Russia, in 1997! Fossils and cave drawings show us that woolly mammoths had long noses and tusks like today's elephants. They reached up to 14 feet (4 m) tall and weighed up to 8 tons (7 t). Three inches (7.6 cm) of fat, two layers of fur, and an overcoat of thick, shaggy hair kept the woolly mammoth warm.

1

Begin by drawing an oval lengthwise. This is the body.

2

Draw a circle on top of the oval as shown. This is the head.

3

For the trunk, draw long, curvy lines that extend from the head.

4

Now draw the shape extending from the head as shown. This is the basic shape of the tusks.

5

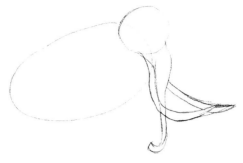

Continue drawing tusks as shown.

6

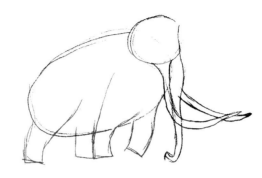

Draw four legs as shown.

7

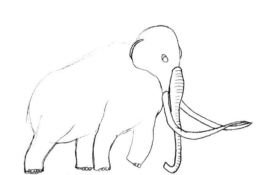

Add detail to the drawing. Draw the toes, ear, eye, and lines in the trunk.

8

Shade the woolly mammoth. Draw single lines to create the look of fur. Draw the lines lightly and at a slight angle. Notice some areas should be shaded more darkly than other areas.

25

Mount McKinley

Seventeen of the twenty highest peaks in the United States are in the state of Alaska. Mount McKinley is the tallest mountain in North America at 20,320 feet (6.2 km) above sea level. The mountain was named after President William McKinley in 1897. President McKinley was the U.S. president from 1897 to 1901. Before that the mountain was called Denali. *Denali* means "the High One" in Athapascan, a North American Indian language spoken in some parts of Alaska. Today the park where Mount McKinley stands is called Denali National Park. During the summer, when the weather is warm and sunny, Mount McKinley's peaks are covered with snow!

1

Begin by drawing a long, curved shape to either end of your paper. This is the basic shape of the mountain.

2

Draw more curves within the shape that you just drew.

3

Begin to draw lines in the mountain. These are the different peaks in the mountain.

4

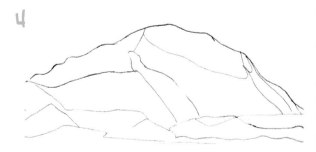

Continue to draw lines in the mountain as shown. Don't worry about getting it perfect. These lines are just here to guide you later when you begin to shade.

5

Continue adding those lines in the mountain.

6

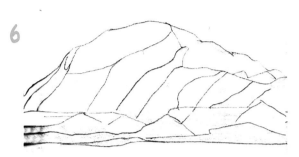

Begin shading very lightly in the areas indicated. Hold your pencil on its side and gently stroke the paper.

7

Shade in a little darker over the areas as shown. Press a little harder on your pencil as you shade those areas.

8

Finish the drawing by shading in the darkest areas as shown. Great job!

27

Alaska's Capitol

The Alaska state capitol is located in Juneau, the state's capital city. Construction for the building began on September 18, 1929, and was completed on February 2, 1931. The four columns that stand in front of the square, concrete building are made of

marble brought from quarries in Tokeen, Alaska, on Prince of Wales Island. The building has six floors. On the lower two floors, the outside of the building has a limestone facade, or front. Men and women who work for the state senate and state house of representatives work in the building.

1

Begin by drawing a long rectangle. This is the base of the capitol.

2

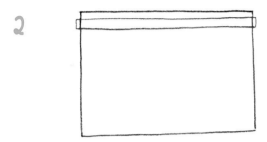

Draw a thin, horizontal rectangle on top as shown. This rectangle should be a little longer than the first rectangle.

3

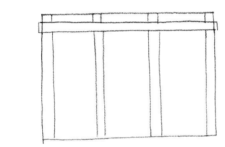

For the columns, draw vertical lines as shown. Notice how they extend past the thin, horizontal rectangle.

4

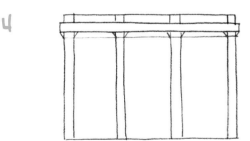

Draw a horizontal line lightly underneath the thin, horizontal rectangle. Use this horizontal line as a guide and draw angled lines that extend from the top of the columns as shown. These lines add detail to the columns.

5

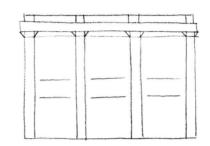

For the windows and the doors, start by drawing short, horizontal lines as shown.

6

Draw vertical lines that extend to the top and bottom of the rectangle to complete the doors and windows.

7

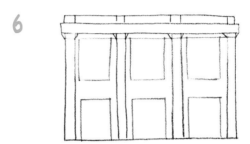

Draw rectangles with triangles on top. Draw T shapes in the center of each window.

8

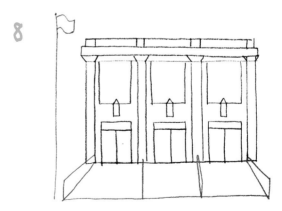

Draw angled lines extending from the bottom of the rectangle as shown. These are the stairs. Add a tall flag.

Alaska State Facts

Statehood	January 3, 1959, 49th state
Area	615,230 square miles (1,593,438 sq km)
State Population	619,500
Capital	Juneau, population, 29,800
Most Populated City	Anchorage, population, 250,500
Industries	Petroleum and natural gas, gold and other mining, food processing, lumber and wood products, tourism
Agriculture	Seafood, nursery stock, dairy products, vegetables, livestock
Motto	North to the Future
Nicknames	The Great Land, The Last Frontier
Flower	Forget-me-not
Bird	Willow ptarmigan
Fossil	Woolly mammoth
Tree	Sitka spruce
Mineral	Gold
Sport	Dog mushing (dog sledding)
Gem	Jade
Marine Mammal	Bowhead whale
Song	"Alaska's Flag"
Land Mammal	Moose
Insect	Four-spot skimmer dragonfly

Glossary

constellation (kon-stuh-LAY-shun) A group of stars.

facade (fuh-SAHD) The front of the building.

flocks (FLOKS) Groups of birds.

glaciers (glay-SHURZ) Large masses of ice in very cold regions or on the tops of high mountains.

limestone (LYM-stohn) A rock that is formed from shells and skeletons.

migrate (MY-grayt) To move from one place to another.

peninsula (puh-NIN-suh-luh) A piece of land mostly surrounded by water but still connected to a larger piece of land.

perennial (peh-REH-nee-ul) Growing for several years without having to be replanted.

population (pop-yoo-LAY-shun) The number of people living in a particular place.

represent (reh-prih-ZENT) To stand for.

shading (SHAYD-ing) The use of colors to show shadows in a drawing.

Siberia (sy-BEER-ee-ah) An area in the country of Russia.

Index

A
Aleutian Islands, 4

B
Benson, Benny, 14

C
capitol, 28

D
Denali National Park, 26

G
Great Land, the, 6

K
Katmai National Park and Preserve, 4
Klondike gold rush, 14

L
Last Frontier, The, 4
Laurence, Sydney, 8, 9

M
McKinley, President William, 26
Mount McKinley, 26

S
salmon, 4, 22
Sitka National Historic Park, 4
state bird, 20
state flag, 14
state flower, 16
state seal, 12

Web Sites

To learn more about Alaska, check out these Web sites:
www.juneau.com/kids/
www.state.ak.us